THE MURD   LIBBY, HOW JUSTICE FOUND RICHARD ALLEN

HOW TWO FRIENDS IN DELPHI WERE LOST AND A COMMUNITY NEVER STOPPED SEARCHING FOR ANSWERS

BY

JULIANNA NEWMAN

COPYRIGHT ©

DISCLAIMER

Please note that the information in this document is provided for informational purposes only. Every effort has been made to present accurate, current, reliable, and complete information. However, no guarantees of any kind are stated or implied. Readers acknowledge that the content of this book is derived from various sources. By reading this document, the reader agrees that the author is not liable, under any circumstances, for any direct or indirect losses arising from the use of the information provided, including but not limited to errors, omissions, or inaccuracies.

TABLE OF CONTENT

The Victims

Background of Abby and Libby

Abigail Williams, known to friends and family as Abby, was thirteen years old and described as a cheerful, creative, and kind-hearted girl who loved sports and art. She was deeply interested in photography and enjoyed spending time outdoors, especially with her best friend, Liberty German. Abby was a promising athlete, participating in volleyball and softball, and she had a vibrant personality that brought joy to those around her. She shared a close relationship with her family and friends, who remember her as a warm and outgoing young girl who brought laughter and positivity into their lives.

Liberty German, known as Libby, was fourteen years old and equally beloved by her community. She was known for her intelligence, curiosity, and maturity beyond her years. Libby excelled academically and had a passion for science, dreaming of one day becoming a scientist. Like Abby, she was also involved in athletics, especially in softball, and was active in her school.

Libby was very close to her family, particularly her older sister, Kelsi, and her grandparents, who were an important part of her life. Known for her resilience and bravery, it was her quick thinking that led to her capturing crucial evidence on her phone, evidence that would eventually become central to the case. Together, Abby and Libby shared a deep friendship, filled with shared interests, laughter, and countless memories. Their bond was unbreakable, and they were often inseparable, spending time together in the small, close-knit community of Delphi, which adored both girls for their spirited and joyful presence.

Delphi, Indiana: A Close-Knit Community

Delphi, Indiana, is a small rural town nestled in Carroll County, with a tight-knit community where neighbors often feel like extended family. With a population of about 3,000 people, Delphi is a place where people form deep roots, and generations of families have lived and grown there, fostering a strong sense of belonging. The town is known for its picturesque landscapes, featuring scenic trails, historical landmarks, and a peaceful rural charm that locals deeply appreciate. The

Monon High Bridge Trail, where Abby and Libby were last seen, is one of the town's well-loved landmarks, often enjoyed by residents and visitors alike. Delphi's close connections and quiet environment are a source of pride for its people, who value the tight bonds that make it feel safe and supportive.

When Abby and Libby's lives were tragically taken, the community was shaken to its core, and their absence left a profound void. Yet, rather than retreating in grief, Delphi rallied together with a resilience and solidarity that demonstrated the strength of its connections. Vigils, fundraisers, and memorials became ways for the town to channel its sorrow and determination to honor the girls and find justice. Families placed orange porch lights in memory of Abby and Libby, symbolizing the ongoing hope for answers. As the investigation unfolded, Delphi's residents became an integral part of efforts to support the girls' families and keep attention on the case. The tragedy bonded the town even more tightly, showing the depth of compassion within a community that has come together to ensure Abby and Libby are never forgotten.

The Friendship Between Abby and Libby

Abby and Libby shared a close and inseparable bond, with a friendship that had grown over years spent together in school, sports, and shared hobbies. Both were young, full of energy, and had a mutual love for outdoor adventures, making the trails around Delphi a favorite place to spend time. They encouraged each other's interests—Libby's passion for science and photography and Abby's love for art and athletics—and brought out the best in one another. Their families often described them as inseparable, two friends who complemented each other and had an easy, natural connection that felt like family. Together, they shared countless memories, laughter, and the typical ups and downs of adolescence, leaning on each other through everything.

Their bond was not only evident to their families but also well-known within the Delphi community. Classmates, teachers, and friends often saw them side-by-side, always eager for new experiences and challenges. Both were active in their school's activities and sports, like softball, which strengthened their friendship further. Their time together was filled with shared dreams and ambitions, and they were known for their kindness, humor, and warmth. In many ways, Abby and Libby were like sisters, supporting each other in every way. Their deep, meaningful friendship has become an enduring part of their legacy, and remembering that bond has provided comfort to their families and the community, which mourns not only two young lives lost but a friendship that held so much love and potential.

The Day of the Disappearance
The Hike on Monon High Bridge Trail

On the afternoon of February 13, 2017, Abby and Libby set out for a hike on the Monon High Bridge Trail, a popular local trail in Delphi, Indiana. The two girls were dropped off by Libby's older sister, Kelsi, at approximately 1:35 p.m., with plans to enjoy the scenic views and capture photos. The trail, which includes the abandoned Monon High Bridge, spans a picturesque but isolated area, making it a favored spot for outdoor activities among residents. At 2:07 p.m., Libby posted a photo of Abby walking along the bridge, which would be the last known sighting of the girls.

As the afternoon passed, Abby and Libby were expected to meet Libby's father at a designated time, but they failed to arrive, prompting immediate concern. After trying to locate them on their own, the families reported the girls missing around 5:30 p.m., and law enforcement soon joined the search. Although authorities initially hoped the girls had merely wandered off, their concern grew overnight. The next day, on February 14, searchers discovered Abby and Libby's bodies in a secluded area roughly half a mile from the bridge. The hike on Monon High Bridge Trail, meant to be an innocent afternoon adventure, marked the beginning of a devastating tragedy that would leave an indelible mark on the community.

The discovery shocked the searchers and devastated the families and community, who had held out hope for a different outcome. Authorities quickly secured the scene and began treating it as a potential crime site. Although officials did not immediately release details about the cause of death or condition of the bodies, the location and circumstances indicated that foul play was involved. This discovery marked the beginning of a long and complex investigation that would eventually capture national attention, as law enforcement searched for answers to this devastating crime.

Initial Law Enforcement Response

When the bodies of Abby and Libby were discovered on February 14, 2017, law enforcement swiftly moved to secure the area, treating it as an active crime scene.

Local police, Carroll County officials, and the Indiana State Police all mobilized to begin a thorough investigation. Recognizing the severity of the case, they brought in specialized resources, including forensic teams, to carefully examine the site for evidence. Officials were tight-lipped about specific findings at the scene, choosing to withhold details from the public to avoid compromising the investigation.

In the days that followed, law enforcement requested assistance from the FBI and other agencies to help manage the high-profile case. They immediately began collecting witness statements, tips, and any relevant information from the community. Within days, police released a grainy photo of a man captured on Libby's phone, which they identified as the primary suspect. Additionally, they shared an audio clip, also recorded on Libby's phone, of a man instructing the girls to go "down the hill." This evidence became central to the investigation and was released to the public in hopes that someone might recognize the suspect. The immediate response by law enforcement underscored the urgency and complexity of the case, launching what would become a years-long search for justice.

Early Theories and Suspicion of Foul Play

In the initial days following the discovery of Abby and Libby's bodies, law enforcement quickly determined that foul play was involved due to the nature of the crime scene. While specific details about how the girls died were withheld, authorities made it clear that this was being investigated as a double homicide. The release of evidence from Libby's phone strongly suggested that they had encountered their killer on the trail. This evidence led to early theories that the suspect was familiar with the Monon High Bridge area and might even be a local resident.

Investigators initially considered a range of possibilities, including the chance that the killer could have been a stranger passing through or, conversely, someone within the Delphi community. The image of the man on the bridge and the phrase "down the hill" became focal points in public speculation and theory development. With limited clues and no immediate suspects, law enforcement cast a wide net, exploring tips and leads from all over the country. The mystery surrounding the photo and audio clip heightened public anxiety, fueling widespread speculation about who the "Bridge Guy" might be and what had led to this tragic outcome on a quiet trail in Delphi.

Evidence Found

The "Bridge Guy" Image and Video

The still image, taken from the video, shows a Caucasian male with his head down, hands in pockets, walking along the bridge toward the girls. His clothing is distinctive: a dark blue jacket, jeans, and a cap. This grainy image, though limited in clarity, was quickly released by law enforcement in the hopes that someone might recognize him.

In addition to the image, Libby recorded a brief audio clip where the man's voice can be heard saying, "Down the hill." This phrase, though simple, provided crucial context and was played repeatedly by investigators to help the public become familiar with the suspect's voice. The combination of the image and audio became vital pieces of evidence, widely circulated on news channels and social media. These clues, though hauntingly limited, reinforced Libby's courage in attempting to capture information about the man who would later be identified as the primary suspect in the case.

Composite Sketches and Suspect Descriptions

Initial Sketches and Public Appeal

In the early days of the Delphi investigation, law enforcement released a composite sketch of a man they identified as a person of interest in the murders of Abby Williams and Libby German. This initial sketch was based on witness accounts and was distributed widely, with officials urging the public to study it closely. Authorities hoped that someone might recognize the man or recall seeing him in the area around the time of the crime. The public appeal, combined with the image of the "Bridge Guy" from Libby's phone, generated significant media coverage and led to thousands of tips.

In April 2019, more than two years after the murders of Abby Williams and Libby German, law enforcement released an updated sketch of the suspect, marking a significant shift in the investigation. This new sketch depicted a younger-looking man, distinctly different from the original sketch initially circulated in 2017. Investigators described this revised image as their primary suspect, suggesting it better represented the individual seen on the Monon High Bridge the day of the murders.

Officials urged the public to examine the new sketch closely, believing the suspect could be someone familiar with Delphi or possibly residing in or around the community. They emphasized that the person might be hiding in plain sight, blending into daily life in the area. The release of this updated sketch sparked renewed interest in the case, generating another wave of tips as people across the nation studied the new image and revisited any information they had previously overlooked.

Theories on the Suspect's Connection to Delphi

As the investigation into the Delphi murders progressed, law enforcement and the public speculated that the suspect might have a connection to Delphi, Indiana. Theories emerged suggesting that the killer could be someone familiar with the Monon High Bridge Trail and the secluded areas surrounding it, given the location of the crime scene. Authorities emphasized that the individual might know the local terrain well enough to choose an isolated spot and evade detection, hinting at a possible link to the community. This belief was further reinforced when officials stated that the suspect might be "hiding in plain sight" and urged residents to consider if someone they knew could match the descriptions and sketches provided.

Additionally, the fact that the suspect seemed comfortable enough to walk along the trail without hesitation led some to believe he might either live in Delphi or frequently visit the area. This theory gained traction following the release of the 2019 updated sketch, which appeared to depict a younger, perhaps more familiar face. Community members and investigators alike considered the possibility that the killer could be a local resident or someone with close ties to the town, making the case all the more unsettling for those living in Delphi.

The Investigation Continues

Police Efforts and Persistence

Since the beginning of the Delphi murders investigation, law enforcement displayed relentless dedication to solving the case, involving multiple agencies, including the Indiana State Police, Carroll County Sheriff's Office, and the FBI. Despite limited evidence, officials worked tirelessly, analyzing thousands of tips, following countless leads, and conducting interviews over the years. They held numerous press conferences to provide updates and urged the public to continue submitting any information that might help identify the suspect.

In addition to standard investigative procedures, police revisited the evidence repeatedly, refining their approach as new information emerged. This included releasing updated sketches and, later, sharing that they had focused on specific suspects who ultimately didn't yield conclusive results. Their persistence was evident even years after the murders, culminating in the arrest of Richard Allen in October 2022, nearly six years after the crime. This tireless effort demonstrated law enforcement's commitment to finding justice for Abby and Libby and the dedication of officers who refused to let the case go cold despite the challenges and lengthy timeline.

Notable Suspects and Leads that Didn't Materialize

Throughout the Delphi investigation, several notable suspects and leads emerged but ultimately didn't lead to a resolution. Early on, law enforcement explored various individuals who matched the general appearance of the "Bridge Guy" or who had a criminal history that raised suspicions. Several men were publicly named or investigated based on physical resemblance to the initial sketches and known behavioral patterns. Despite these apparent connections, none of these suspects provided the evidence needed to charge them, and they were later ruled out.

Additionally, tips from across the nation pointed to potential leads, some linking the case to other crimes or suggesting that the killer might be a transient or someone from outside the area. Investigators diligently pursued each tip, conducting interviews and background checks, but these leads ultimately did not yield any breakthroughs.

Richard Allen's Arrest

Discovery of the Misfiled Tip

In 2022, a breakthrough in the Delphi murders investigation came when a misfiled tip led investigators to Richard Allen, a Delphi resident who had already been interviewed shortly after Abby and Libby's deaths. Three days after the murders, Allen had voluntarily come forward, stating that he was on the Monon High Bridge Trail on the day the girls disappeared. He reported seeing them on the trail but claimed he did not interact with them. However, this tip was somehow misfiled in the early stages of the investigation, preventing it from being thoroughly examined at the time.

The tip resurfaced during a review of the case by a volunteer file clerk who uncovered the overlooked statement. This rediscovery shifted the investigation's focus back to Allen, prompting a closer examination of his story and background. Investigators re-interviewed him and uncovered further evidence, including the match between an unspent bullet found at the crime scene and a gun he owned. This discovery of the misfiled tip became a critical turning point, finally leading to Allen's arrest and charges, nearly six years after the murders.

Police Surveillance and Collection of Evidence

After Richard Allen's resurfaced 2017 statement positioned him as a key suspect, police began discreet surveillance to gather additional evidence linking him to the Delphi murders. Investigators monitored Allen's activities and interactions while building a case to connect him directly to the crime scene. During this time, they examined his background and conducted forensic analyses of items associated with him, including a .40-caliber firearm he owned, which became a central piece of evidence.

Forensic testing revealed that an unspent .40-caliber round found near the bodies of Abby and Libby matched Allen's gun, which had been in his possession since 2001. This discovery significantly strengthened the case, as the bullet was located between the victims at the crime scene. The link between the ammunition and Allen's weapon provided the tangible evidence investigators had been seeking for years, ultimately leading to Allen's arrest and charges in October 2022.

Legal Proceedings and Gag Orders

Initial Charges and Court Orders

In October 2022, Richard Allen was formally charged with two counts of murder in connection with the deaths of Abby Williams and Libby German. This arrest marked a major development in the Delphi case, which had remained unsolved for nearly six years. Following his arrest, Allen pleaded not guilty to the charges, maintaining his innocence as the legal process began. Given the high-profile nature of the case and intense public interest, the court implemented several protective measures to ensure a fair trial.

Judge Frances Gull issued a gag order shortly after the charges, limiting what attorneys, law enforcement, and other officials could publicly discuss about the case. This order aimed to prevent pretrial publicity from influencing potential jurors and to protect the integrity of the upcoming trial.

The Motion to Move the Trial

Richard Allen's defense team filed a motion to move the trial out of Carroll County, arguing that the extensive local media coverage and the emotional impact of the case within the small Delphi community could prevent a fair and impartial jury from being selected. Given the national attention on the case and the tight-knit nature of Delphi, the defense expressed concern that finding unbiased jurors locally would be challenging, as many potential jurors might already have formed opinions about Allen's guilt or innocence.

In response, the court considered the request, recognizing the potential influence of the widespread publicity surrounding the murders. The defense sought a venue that would provide a broader pool of jurors who might not be as familiar with the case details. This motion was part of the defense's broader strategy to ensure that Allen received a fair trial, untainted by the intense scrutiny and emotional responses from Delphi residents who had closely followed the case for years.

The Defense's Arguments and Community Concerns

The defense team for Richard Allen argued that he would struggle to receive a fair trial in Carroll County due to the deep emotional connection of the local community to the Delphi murders and the intense media coverage surrounding the case. They claimed that the years of public interest, coupled with the release of key evidence like the "Bridge Guy" video and sketches, had likely shaped public opinion, making it challenging to find unbiased jurors in the area. The defense also highlighted the public's strong reactions and theories shared on social media, further complicating the atmosphere for an impartial trial.

Meanwhile, community members expressed both relief at the arrest and concern about the legal process. Many in Delphi wanted justice for Abby and Libby but were wary about how the extended media exposure might impact the case's outcome. There was a general hope that the trial would proceed fairly and that the intense public interest would not interfere with the justice process. The balance between the defense's push for a fair trial and the community's desire for resolution reflected the complicated emotions surrounding this case.

Pre-Trial Developments and Evidence Unsealed

Allen's Confessions and Statements

While in custody, Richard Allen allegedly made over 60 confessions to the murders of Abby Williams and Libby German, according to statements presented by prosecutors. These admissions were reportedly made to multiple individuals, including his wife, mother, prison staff, fellow inmates, and even in conversations with a prison psychologist. The confessions were shared in various forms, including in-person conversations, phone calls, and written statements. Allen's statements were consistent in admitting his role in the killings, reinforcing the prosecution's case against him.

Prosecutors argued that these repeated admissions were reliable and highlighted Allen's awareness of his actions. They also included specific details of the crime, which only someone with direct involvement would know, adding weight to the evidence. The defense challenged the credibility of these statements, raising concerns about Allen's mental health and questioning the conditions under which some of these confessions were allegedly made. However, the sheer volume and consistency of Allen's statements became a central element of the prosecution's argument for his guilt.

Witness Accounts of Allen's Movements

Witness accounts placed Richard Allen on the Monon High Bridge Trail around the time of Abby and Libby's disappearance, reinforcing suspicions about his presence in the area. One witness reported seeing a man matching Allen's description—wearing a blue jacket and jeans—walking away from the trail that afternoon. The witness noted that the man appeared "muddy and bloody," suggesting he had been in a struggle or traversed rough terrain.

Another witness observed a car parked near the trailhead in an unusual manner, with the license plate partially obscured, matching a vehicle Allen was known to drive in 2017. These observations aligned with Allen's own statement, where he admitted being on the trail that day. These witness accounts provided additional support to the prosecution's case by corroborating Allen's proximity to the crime scene and raising questions about his activities in the area around the time of the murders.

The Trial of Richard Allen

Jury Selection and Trial Preparation

The jury selection process for Richard Allen's trial was meticulous, given the widespread publicity surrounding the Delphi murders. The defense and prosecution sought to ensure an impartial jury, screening potential jurors to gauge their exposure to media coverage and any preconceived opinions about Allen's guilt or innocence. Due to concerns about local bias, some jurors were selected from outside Carroll County to help mitigate the influence of community sentiment on the trial's outcome.

In preparation for the trial, both sides reviewed extensive evidence, including forensic reports, witness statements, and Allen's alleged confessions. The prosecution focused on building a clear narrative connecting Allen to the crime scene, particularly with the forensic match to the .40 caliber bullet. Meanwhile, the defense prepared to challenge the reliability of witness accounts and Allen's statements, citing potential mental health issues as a factor. This careful preparation underscored the complexity and high stakes of the case, as both sides aimed to present a thorough, compelling argument to the jury.

Graphic Details of the Murders Presented in Court

In court, prosecutors shared graphic details about the murders of Abby Williams and Libby German, which underscored the brutality of the crime. They revealed that both girls had their throats cut, describing the injuries in a way that conveyed the violence of the attack. Prosecutors stated that Abby was found fully clothed, while Libby's body was discovered unclothed, which pointed to the possibility of an attempted sexual assault, though they did not confirm this as a conclusive motive.

These details, though difficult for the families and community to hear, were presented as essential aspects of the case to demonstrate the intent and severity of the crime. By presenting this evidence, the prosecution aimed to convey the horror of the murders to the jury framing the crime as deliberate and heinous. The disturbing nature of the injuries and crime scene description reinforced the gravity of the charges against Richard Allen, contributing to the case that he was responsible for the killings.

Psychological Insights and Defense Arguments

Defense's Psychological Profile of Allen

The defense presented a psychological profile of Richard Allen, arguing that his mental health issues could affect the credibility of his alleged confessions. A clinical psychologist testified that Allen had been diagnosed with severe depression, anxiety, and other mental health conditions, which may have influenced his behavior and statements. They argued that his confessions in custody might not have been reliable, as his mental state could lead to confusion or misinterpretation of events.

Additionally, the defense brought in a neuropsychologist who discussed Allen's work-related stress and personal struggles, highlighting the psychological toll these factors could have had on him. The defense's goal was to present Allen as a man under considerable mental strain, suggesting that his confessions could have been the result of psychological instability rather than a clear admission of guilt. This psychological profile was intended to create reasonable doubt regarding the reliability of the prosecution's evidence and Allen's state of mind during the alleged confessions.

Prosecutors' Arguments on Allen as "Bridge Guy"

Prosecutors argued that Richard Allen was the man known as "Bridge Guy," the suspect captured on Libby German's phone approaching the girls on the Monon High Bridge. They presented evidence linking Allen to the scene, including the .40 caliber bullet found near the bodies that matched Allen's gun. Additionally, a State Police Master Trooper testified that Allen's voice was consistent with the "down the hill" command heard in the audio clip recorded by Libby, directly associating him with the suspect's voice.

The prosecution also highlighted witness testimonies placing a man matching Allen's description near the trail on the day of the murders. By combining the physical evidence, witness accounts, and the voice identification, prosecutors aimed to build a compelling case that Allen was indeed "Bridge Guy." Thei argument centered on connecting these multiple points of evidence to position Allen as the individual responsible for the murders of Abby and Libby, urging the jury to see him as the person in the video and audio recording from that day.

Verdict and Aftermath

The Jury's Deliberation

The jury in Richard Allen's trial began their deliberations on November 7, 2024, after hearing weeks of detailed testimonies and examining critical evidence linking Allen to the murders of Abby Williams and Libby German. They reviewed key points presented by both the prosecution and defense, including the .40 caliber bullet found at the scene, Allen's alleged confessions, witness accounts, and mental health evaluations that raised questions about the reliability of his statements.

Jurors faced the task of weighing the prosecution's evidence tying Allen to the crime against the defense's arguments on his mental health and the credibility of his confessions. Deliberations continued for several days, reflecting the gravity and complexity of the case. On November 11, 2024, the jury reached a unanimous verdict, finding Richard Allen guilty on all counts related to the murders, bringing a significant resolution to a case that had haunted the Delphi community for years.

Richard Allen's Conviction on November 11, 2024

On November 11, 2024, Richard Allen was found guilty on all counts for the murders of Abby Williams and Libby German, concluding a trial that had captivated and deeply affected the Delphi community. The jury's unanimous verdict came after days of deliberation, during which they assessed critical evidence, including the .40 caliber bullet linked to Allen's gun, his alleged confessions, and witness testimonies placing him at the scene. This conviction marked a significant closure in a case that had remained unsolved for nearly seven years, offering a long-awaited sense of justice for the families and community.

Allen's conviction reaffirmed the prosecution's argument that he was the individual known as "Bridge Guy," captured in the video and audio evidence recorded by Libby on the day of the murders. With the guilty verdict, the court scheduled a sentencing hearing for December 20, where Allen faces the possibility of a life sentence. For the families of Abby and Libby, the verdict brought a measure of resolution, though the emotional scars of the tragedy remain.

Lessons Learned and Reflections on Justice

Law Enforcement and Legal Takeaways

The Delphi murder case highlighted several key takeaways for law enforcement and the legal system, emphasizing the importance of thorough evidence management and community collaboration. The resurfacing of Richard Allen's 2017 tip, which had been misfiled, underscored the need for meticulous record-keeping in major investigations. This oversight delayed a significant lead for years, demonstrating the potential consequences of procedural errors in high-stakes cases.

The case also reinforced the value of public involvement, as the consistent tips and community vigilance helped sustain the investigation over time. Legally, the trial showcased the challenges of balancing public interest with fair trial rights, leading to gag orders and motions for a venue change to maintain impartiality. The conviction illustrated the impact of combining forensic evidence, such as the matching .40 caliber bullet, with digital and witness evidence. These takeaways are likely to influence future investigations, reminding law enforcement and legal professionals of the critical role of organization, forensic detail, and public partnership in complex cases.

Family Statements on Justice and Closure

Following Richard Allen's conviction, the families of Abby Williams and Libby German expressed a mix of relief and sorrow. They acknowledged that while the guilty verdict provided a sense of justice, it could never fully heal the pain of losing their daughters. In their statements, both families emphasized gratitude for the tireless efforts of law enforcement, the support from the Delphi community, and the resilience of those who stood by them throughout the seven-year ordeal.

They also spoke about a measure of closure, knowing the person responsible for the murders was held accountable, yet they recognized that closure does not erase the void left by Abby and Libby's absence. The families hoped that the conviction would allow them and the community to begin moving forward, honoring the girls' memories while finding a way to heal. Their statements reflected a deep appreciation for the justice achieved, tempered by the enduring grief of their loss.

The Lasting Legacy of Abby and Libby

Contributions of the L & A Park Foundation

The L & A Park Foundation, established to honor the lives of Abby Williams and Libby German, has made significant contributions to the Delphi community by developing the Abby and Libby Memorial Park. This park features amenities such as an amphitheater, three baseball/softball fields, picnic shelters, two playgrounds, and walking trails across 20 acres, providing a space for recreation and community gatherings.

In 2020, the foundation was recognized as a recipient of the NBA All-Star 2021 Legacy Grant, which supported the park's development and programming. Through these efforts, the L & A Park Foundation has created a lasting tribute to Abby and Libby, fostering a sense of community and providing a place for appreciation of nature, art, play, and athleticism for generations to come.

In addition, the Delphi Community Middle School, where both girls were students, renamed its library the "Abby and Libby Memorial Library." This dedication ensures that their presence remains a part of the school they once attended, inspiring future generations. Each year, local events and fundraisers are held in their memory, with proceeds supporting the park and other community initiatives. These memorials stand as a testament to Abby and Libby's enduring legacy, allowing family, friends, and residents to remember them with love and ensure they are never forgotten.

Conclusion

Final Thoughts on the Delphi Case

The Delphi case stands as both a heartbreaking tragedy and a testament to perseverance in the face of uncertainty. For nearly seven years, the families of Abby Williams and Libby German, supported by the Delphi community and a dedicated team of investigators, held onto hope for justice. The case highlighted the importance of community involvement, with public tips and national attention keeping the investigation active. Richard Allen's conviction brought a sense of resolution, marking the end of a long and complex legal journey.

While justice has been served, the case leaves a lasting impact on Delphi, reminding the town of the precious lives lost and the importance of vigilance and unity. Abby and Libby's legacy continues through the park and community initiatives, symbols of remembrance that honor their lives. The Delphi case underscores the power of resilience and collective determination, showing how a community can rally together to seek justice and healing in the face of profound loss.

The Future of the Delphi Community

The Delphi community, while forever marked by the tragedy of Abby Williams and Libby German's deaths, looks toward the future with a focus on healing and unity. The Abby and Libby Memorial Park has become a central part of this effort, offering a place for residents to gather, reflect, and celebrate the lives of the two girls. This park and other community initiatives continue to strengthen the bonds among residents, emphasizing resilience and shared support.

Moving forward, Delphi aims to honor the memory of Abby and Libby by fostering a safe, connected environment for all its residents. The case has heightened community awareness around safety and vigilance, while also reminding the town of the importance of community solidarity. Through remembrance activities and ongoing support for the families, Delphi seeks to build a future that preserves the legacy of Abby and Libby, ensuring they remain an enduring part of the town's spirit.

Made in the USA
Columbia, SC
07 December 2024

48686288R00035